Crafty
EVER AFTER

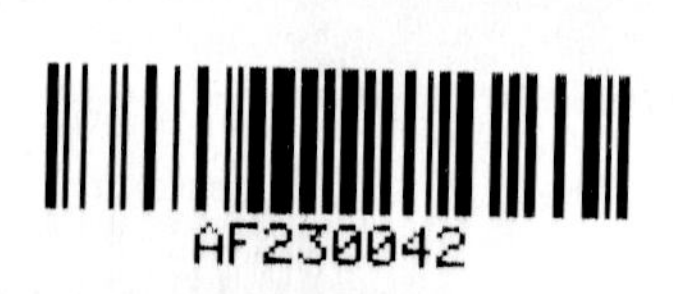

Marbled
E N D P A P E R S
Collection Two

Crafty
EVER AFTER

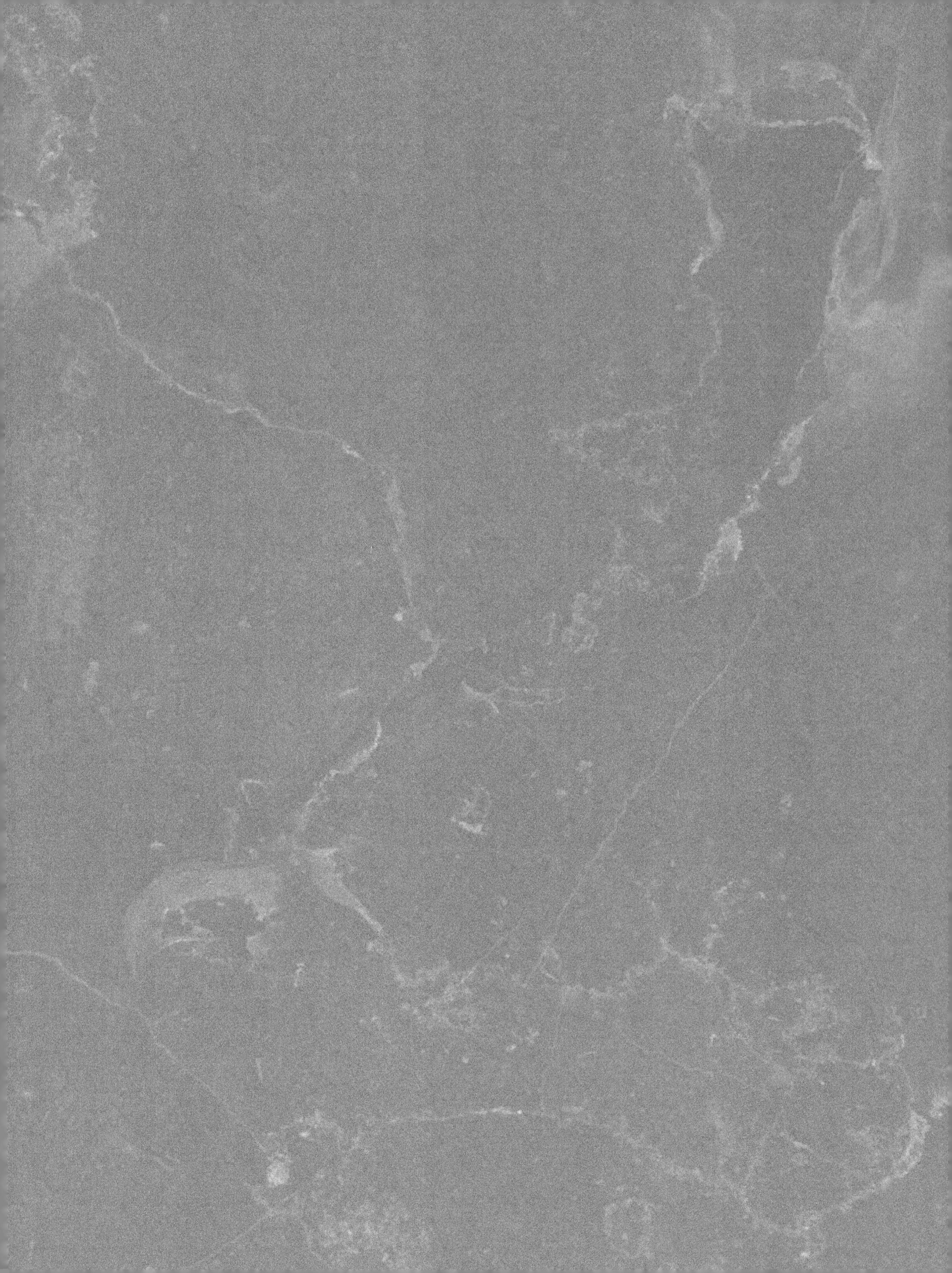

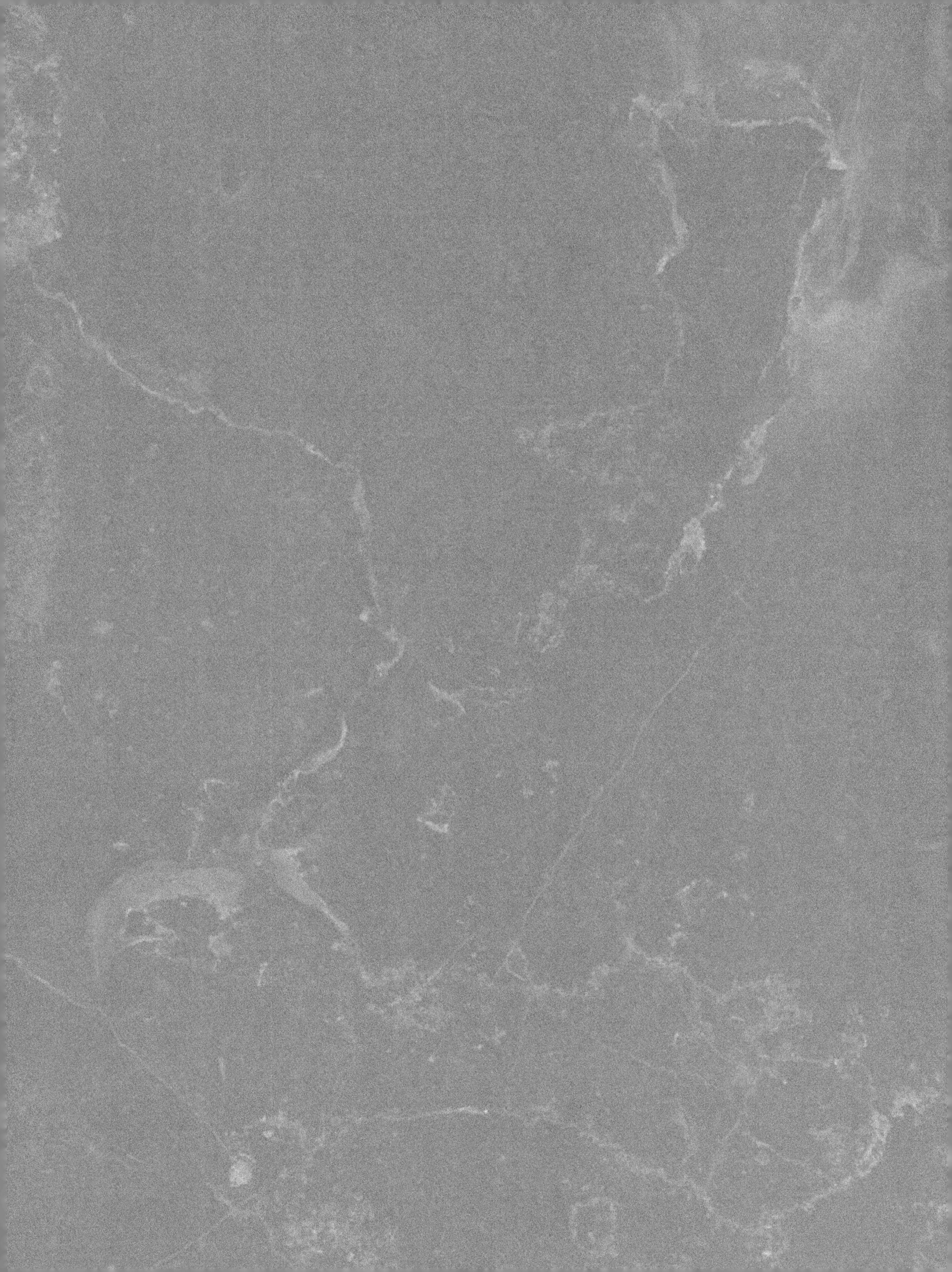